Day and Night

written by Maria Gordon
and
illustrated by Mike Gordon

Thomson Learning

New York

Simple Science

Day and Night
Float and Sink
Fun with Color
Fun with Heat
Fun with Light
Push and Pull

First published in the
United States in 1995 by
Thomson Learning
New York, NY

Published simultaneously in Great Britain
by Wayland (Publishers) Limited

Library of Congress Cataloging-in-Publication Data

Gordon, Maria.
  Day and night / written by Maria Gordon and
illustrated by Mike Gordon.
        p.   cm. — (Simple science)
  Includes bibliographical references and index.
  ISBN 1-56847-457-1 (hc) — ISBN 1-56847-461-X (pbk.)
  1. Day—Juvenile literature. 2. Night—Juvenile literature.
3. Earth—Rotation—Juvenile literature. [1. Day. 2. Night.
3. Earth—Rotation.] I. Gordon, Mike, ill. II. Title.
III. Series: Simple science (New York, N.Y.)
QB633.G67   1995
525'.3—dc20   95-13656

Printed in Italy

12.95

Contents

It is day when the sun lights up
the world around you.

It is night when the world around
you is dark.

Days are light because the sun shines very brightly. We see no sunshine at night, so nights are dark. Most people and many animals and plants are busy in the day and rest at night.

Other animals and plants are busy at night. They are nocturnal. Nocturnal animals can see with very little light, or they use other ways to tell what is around them.

Bats, owls, snails, foxes, badgers, and the other animals you see here are nocturnal.

Animals like tiny shellfish and fireflies make their own light at night so they can find each other!

Some plants, like honeysuckle, have flowers that smell stronger at night. Moths come to feed on them.

Long ago, people saw how the sun gives light to the earth. Some used huge stones to make patterns for the sun to shine through. Many thought the sun was a god. They gave the sun names like Apollo, Ra, and Surya.

People gave names to stars and the other objects they saw in the sky. They learned that they could see different stars from different places. This helped them find their way on long journeys.

The earth is like a giant ball in space. The sun looks smaller, but really it is a much bigger ball that is very far away. The moon really is smaller than the earth but it is much closer to us than the sun is.

This is how
the earth, the
moon, and the sun
would look if you saw them
from a spaceship.

Look out of a window at different times of the day. The sun seems to move across the sky. Ask an adult to help you make a chart showing how the sun seems to move.

10 o'clock

12 O'clock

2 O'clock

9 o'clock

4 O'clock

7 o'clock

6 O'clock

Do this on summer and winter days. The sun seems lower in winter.

Really the earth is moving, not the sun! People used to think that the sun moves around the earth. But scientists named Aristarchus, Copernicus, and Galileo showed that the earth moves around the sun.

Galileo proved it with a telescope. He traced the motion of objects in the sky.

The earth takes one year to go around the sun. But the earth also spins slowly while it goes around the sun.

Ask an adult to help you push a pencil through the middle of an orange. Turn the pencil to make the orange spin. This is how the earth turns while it moves through space.

Ask an adult to put a lamp without a shade in the middle of a table. Turn on the light. (Don't look straight at the bulb.)

Put a red sticker on one side of the orange and a green sticker on the other side. Spin the orange slowly on the edge of the table. First one sticker is lit up, then the other.

The stickers on your orange are like places on different sides of the world. As the earth turns, the sun shines on the places on one side. It is day in these places. The places on the other side of the earth are turned away from the sun. There, it is night.

As the earth keeps turning, the dark places come back into the light. People there can see the sun very low down in the sky. This is called sunrise. It is the beginning of the day.

The earth keeps turning so the sun seems to get higher. The time when the sun is highest in the sky is the middle of the day. This is called noon.

The earth keeps on turning. The daytime places are slowly turned away from the sun. The sun seems to get lower. Then it cannot be seen any more. This is called sunset. It is the end of day and the beginning of night.

Make your orange and pencil lean like this. This is how the earth leans! This means parts of the earth are closer to the sun than others.

These places take longer to turn away from the sun so their days are longer.

The places at the other end of the world are farther away from the sun. These places have very long nights.

21

How long are your days?

Was the sun in the sky
before you got up?

What will you do
after sunset?
What time of year
is it?

Ask an adult to help you make a chart showing how long days last in winter, spring, summer, and autumn. Days are shortest in winter. When it is winter somewhere, that place is farthest from the sun. This is because the earth is leaning away from the sun.

Day is the time between sunrise and sunset. But day is also the name for a whole day and night together!
Spin your orange and pencil once so the stickers end up where they started.
This is like the earth turning once.
The time it takes is called a day.

How many days is it to your birthday? The answer will tell you how many times the Earth will turn until that time.

You cannot feel the earth turning or moving around the sun. It feels as if the earth is still and the sun is moving around the earth.

Unlike the sun, the moon really does move around the earth. It takes twenty nine and one-half days to go completely around. You can see the moon best at night.

The moon looks as if it is shining, but it cannot make its own light. It is lit up by the sun. When the earth is between the sun and the moon, it stops some of the light, so only part of the moon is lit up.

This is why the moon seems to change shape.

People use light to help them work and play. Your eyes need light to see. Sunlight lets you know that it is day. Blind people's eyes do not work. They use special clocks to tell them when it is day or night.

Additional projects

Here are a few more projects to show day and night. The projects go with the pages listed next to them. These projects are harder than the ones in the book, so be sure to ask an adult to help you.

4/5   Discuss where the sun is on cloudy days. The sun shines all the time, but we only see it at certain times of the day. Why? Sunlight contains vitamins, so it is important to get a little sunlight every day. Too much sun can be harmful, though. Find out how much sunlight is healthy.

6/7   With an adult, take a walk at night and the same walk in the daytime. Is it easier to see colors in the daylight? Why? Compare land and sea at night.

8/9   Visit a planetarium. Find out how a sundial is used.

10/11   Make a display of photographs taken in space. Make a painting showing comparative sizes of the sun, the moon, and the earth. Or make a model of the solar system using spheres such as baseballs, marbles, golfballs, and a basketball for the sun.

12/13   Learn how to use telescopes and binoculars. Remember, never look directly at the sun! Investigate the Hubble Space telescope.

14/15   Put a lamp in the middle of a round table. Walk around the table carrying the orange. This is how the earth moves around the sun. Try to spin the orange as you walk around the table to show how a year is divided into days.

16/17   Discuss what time zones are and learn how to find time zones on maps and globes.

18/19   Plot temperatures throughout a sunny day. Watch a sunset.

20/21   Investigate six-month-long nights and days in the Arctic and Antarctic. What kinds of animals can survive in these cold places? What do the people there do to keep warm?

24/25 Spin a globe to show how the earth turns during a day. Shine a flashlight at one spot on the globe. This represents the sun. Shine the light over the town where you live. This is how the sun appears over your town at noon.

26/27 Have an adult show you how the moon appears at different times during its 29-1/2 day turn around the earth. It has four main phases, or shapes: new moon, first quarter, full moon, last quarter. Look at the moon's shape once each week for a month and make cut-outs of the shapes you see. Find out about solar eclipses and lunar eclipses.

28/29 Find out about the things in the pictures on these pages. What is sun screen for? Why do cameras need flashbulbs? Why is it dark in movie theaters? How can we see sporting events played at night, when it is dark?

Other books to read

Gordon, Maria. **Fun with Light.** Simple Science. New York: Thomson Learning, 1995.

Lewellen, J. **Moon, Sun and Stars.** New True Books. Chicago: Childrens Press, 1992.

Richardson, Joy. **Day and Night.** Picture Science. New York: Franklin Watts, 1992.

Suhr, Mandy. **Sight.** Minneapolis: Carolrhoda Books, 1993.

Index